FLYING FORCES

Written by Paul Stevenson

CONTENTS

Air Forces at Work	4
Ready to Act	6
Every Second Counts!	8
Emergency Help	10
Supplies on the Way	12
The Pilots and Gear	14
Flying Techniques	16
G-Force	18
F-35 Fighter Jet	20
Gripen Fighter Jet	22
B-21 Raider	24
Refuelling in the Air	26
Support Aircraft	28
Pilot Training	30
Glossary	31
Index	32

First published in 2024 by
Hungry Tomato Ltd
F15, Old Bakery Studios,
Blewetts Wharf, Malpas Road,
Truro, Cornwall,
TR1 1QH, UK.

Thanks to our editor, Julie Tofflemire.

Copyright © 2024 Hungry Tomato Ltd

No part of this publication may be reproduced, stored in a retrieval system, or transmitted in any form or by any means, electronic, mechanical, photocopying, recording, or otherwise, without prior written permission of the copyright owner.

A CIP catalogue record for this book is available from the British Library.

ISBN 9781835691236
Printed in China

Discover more at
www.hungrytomato.com

Neither the publisher nor the author shall be liable for any bodily harm or damage to property whatsoever that may be caused or sustained as a result of conducting any of the activities featured in this book.

All words in **BOLD** can be found in the glossary.

AIR FORCES AT WORK

Air forces are the pilots and powerful planes that a country uses to guard and defend itself.

In a war, the air force works hard to protect soldiers on the ground from enemy planes. The planes, and the pilots, need to be tough to do this job.

Most countries, as well as **NATO**, have their own air power in some form. The United States has the largest air force in the world, with over 5,000 active aircraft.

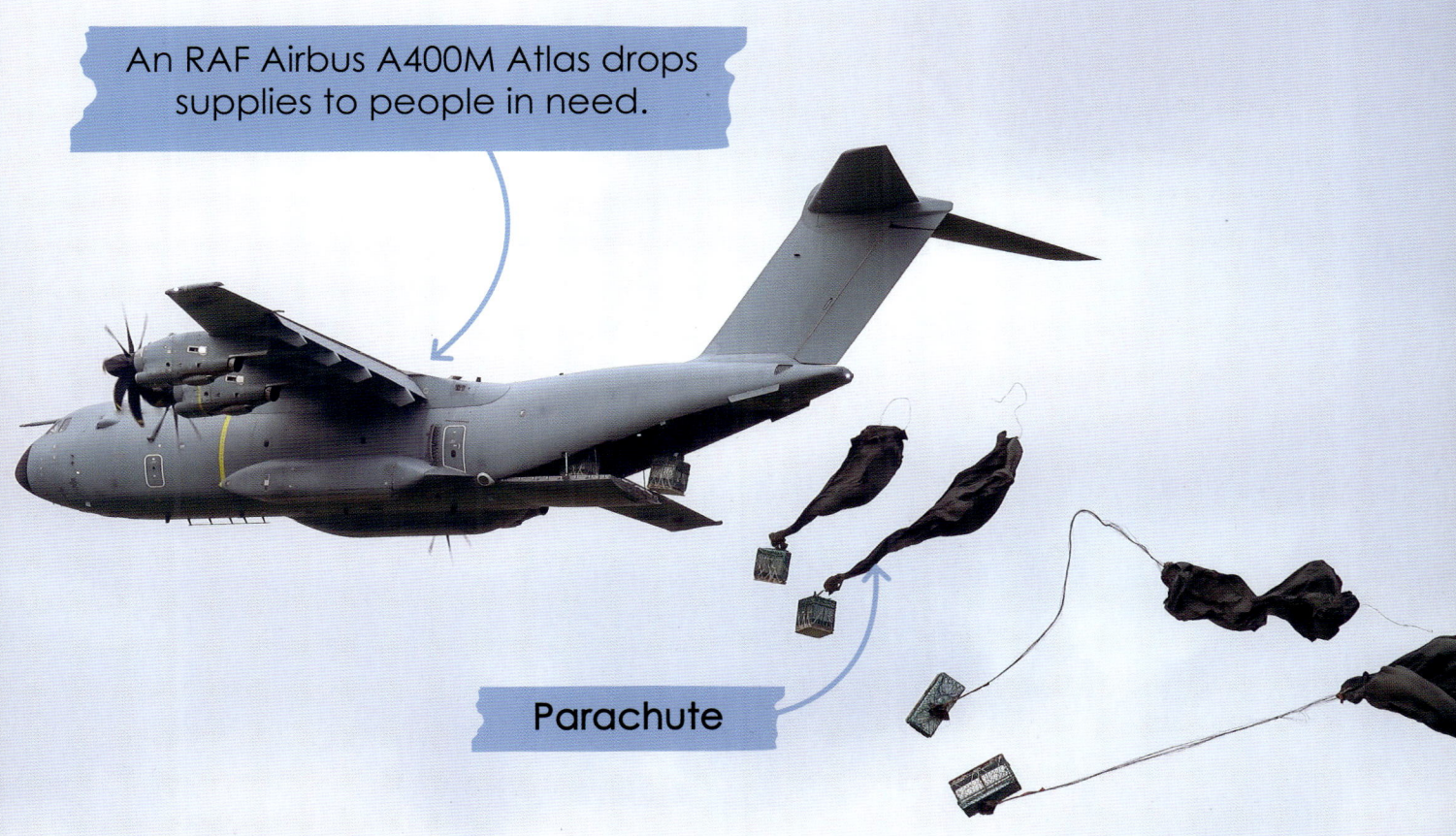

An RAF Airbus A400M Atlas drops supplies to people in need.

Parachute

When not at war, the air force's job is to keep people safe. For example, they try to stop enemy attacks from happening.

Air forces also help people affected by natural disasters such as floods and earthquakes.

READY TO ACT

When something unusual or dangerous happens in a country's **airspace**, fighter plane crews need to be ready.

Every minute of every day there are thousands of aircraft in the air. Controllers on the ground watch the signals sent from aircraft. The controllers also watch for enemy planes flying into their country's airspace.

If the controller spots something unexpected, the fighter plane crews need to check it out.

Controller

The crews are always standing by, ready to take action at a moment's notice. This is a Quick Reaction Alert (QRA), known in the USA as an Airspace Control Alert (ACA). However, most people call it a "scramble".

An F-18 Hornet fighter jet

As the pilots run to their planes, **ground crews** prepare the planes for a quick take-off.

Planes can also be ready to take off from huge ships called aircraft carriers.

EVERY SECOND COUNTS!

Air force crews need to move quickly to stop the threat. Their fast response time can save lives.

To be ready for a scramble, the aircraft are positioned so they can take off easily. The pilots also have to get ready quickly. They even sleep in their flying gear to save time in case they have to scramble!

Within minutes of the alert, the jets are flying.

Fighter jets can **accelerate** at up to 1,535 mph – this is twice the speed of sound!

The pilots fly close to the enemy aircraft to see how dangerous the threat is. Then they report back to the people in charge on the ground, who decide what happens next.

POWERFUL JET ENGINES GIVE THE PLANES INCREDIBLE SPEED!

EMERGENCY HELP

Air forces don't just fight wars and stop enemies. They also help around the world when there is a major emergency.

In December 2023, Chennai, India, was flooded after heavy rains following a major **cyclone**.

The flood caused power to cut out across the city. It also made many roads and train services unusable. The Indian Air Force (IAF) used Chetak helicopters to drop food and medical supplies to people in the area.

In emergencies, the air force can go to places that are hard to reach.

SUPPLIES ON THE WAY

Air forces help to get supplies to people and places that need them. This is especially important when roads are damaged.

In February 2023, two massive earthquakes hit the southern region of Turkey. With **magnitudes** of 7.7 and 7.6, they caused severe damage.

The United States Air Force (USAF) acted quickly to send **first responders** to the people who were affected by the earthquakes.

Air force men and women also helped on the ground. They looked after people who were hurt. They transported supplies and made a huge difference in the recovery efforts.

A C-17 can get lots of **cargo** or people to a site quickly.

A C-17 Globemaster transport plane

THE PILOTS AND GEAR

When not at war, fighter pilots are on duty for QRA/ACA. They also fly training missions called "sorties".

During some sorties, pilots practise flying low to the ground. They also do pretend air-to-air battles! A training flight is two to four hours long. A normal day also includes **intelligence**, weather and weapons **briefings**.

Making pre-flight checks before a sortie.

"Every time we get airborne, we do something to make us better pilots. There is always a point to the sortie."
- **Fighter Pilot Sam Cowan**

FLYING GEAR

Pilots need a lot of special gear to get the job done.

Oxygen mask

Helmet with breather regulator to supply oxygen

Life jacket

One-piece flight suit

Leather flying gloves

Inflatable g-pants

Boots

FLYING TECHNIQUES

Unlike airline pilots, air force pilots are trained to fly at low levels. This is so they can fly planes under enemy radar.

Low-level flying is fast and very dangerous. It needs to be practised regularly. All the flying is done by the pilot. There is no help from computers.

The pilot is flying at 7 miles per minute. The plane is just 46 metres off the ground.

THE SMALLEST MISTAKE COULD MEAN CERTAIN DEATH FOR THE PILOT!

Fighter pilots also need to be prepared for air combat manoeuvring, a battle in the air at close range. This is better known as a dogfight. During a dogfight, pilots try to attack or **evade** other aircraft.

Pilots must think and act quickly during a dogfight.

G-FORCE

Pilots must learn to cope with g-force. G-force is what you feel when you hurtle down a rollercoaster.

As g-force gets higher, it affects the pilot's body. Blood is dragged to the pilot's legs and feet. Special trousers called "g-pants" help to stop this.

Next to go is peripheral vision. This means the pilot can't see out of the corners of his or her eyes. It's like looking down two toilet roll tubes. Finally, everything turns black and white. The pilot may even pass out.

As g-force gets lower, the pilot's senses return to normal.

The g-force on a rollercoaster is about 3g. For a fighter pilot, it can reach up to 9g.

THE AIRCRAFT: F-35 FIGHTER JET

This jet has supreme power, attacking and bombing enemy targets on the ground and in the air.

The F-35's air-to-surface missiles can destroy targets over 200 miles away. With this range, the F-35 can fire a missile before the enemy even knows it's there.

It can also shoot down enemy planes with air-to-air missiles, which are missiles fired from the air at something in the air.

The missiles use a guidance system to find their target.

The F-35 is often called a "flying computer" because of its amazing software. A display system on the pilot's helmet shows information about fuel and **altitude**.

The F-35 has six **infrared cameras**. These cameras help the pilot "see" right through the jet and watch out for incoming missiles.

GRIPEN FIGHTER JET

Sweden's Gripen fighter jet is smaller than many other fighters, but that makes it fast.

It can reach a top speed of over 1,500 mph! It can also take off from regular roads or damaged runways.

In 2018, a forest fire in Sweden had been burning for two weeks. When dropping water didn't work, the Swedish government decided to fight fire with fire...

It sent a Gripen to drop a laser-guided bomb onto the fire. The plan worked!

The Gripen can even stop a forest fire!

B-21 RAIDER

The B-21 is a stealth bomber designed for long-range bombing and nuclear missions.

Sometimes the best way to beat the enemy is to hide from it! The B-21 uses **stealth technology**.

This means it is very hard for enemy radar to **detect** it. The plane has time to make an attack before it is spotted on the enemy's radar.

Radar systems scan for enemy aircraft.

The B-21 can hold two pilots, but it was also designed to be flown remotely. In that case, the person operating the plane would still be on the ground!

The B-21 will slowly replace B-2 bombers like this one.

REFUELLING IN THE AIR

Fighter jets need to be light and fast, so they only carry enough fuel for 60 to 90 minutes of flying. They need to get more fuel while still in the air.

A Combat Air Patrol (CAP) can last for hours. This is when fighter jets patrol an area looking for enemy aircraft. Air-to-air refuelling allows the fighter jets to stay in the air.

Jet taking on fuel

Tanker plane

Large planes act as airborne fuel tankers. Fighter jets waiting for fuel, and those that have been refuelled, protect the tanker plane.

Fuel is delivered using a basket-like piece of equipment on the end of a long hose.

Hose

Basket

SUPPORT AIRCRAFT

Air forces around the world use lots of different support aircraft during wars and rescue missions.

The CH-47 Chinook is a twin-engine, heavy-lift helicopter. Its main job is moving troops and supplies to battlefields.

Tandem rotors

CH-47 Chinook helicopter

The Chinook has a wide loading ramp at the back. In flight, soldiers can parachute from the ramp, or supplies can be dropped.

The C-5M Super Galaxy is the USAF's largest aircraft. It transports cargo and military **personnel**. Its interior cargo compartment is 44 metres long.

The C-5M Super Galaxy can take off with 127,460 kg of cargo.

PILOT TRAINING

BECOME A TRAINEE

To be given a place as a trainee pilot, you must have excellent exam results. You must also be in good shape and have good eyesight. Pilots also need above-average **coordination** skills.

TRAINING

Pilots train on full-motion flight simulators. The simulators handle and respond exactly the same as real aircraft. However, the trainee pilots don't have to leave the ground.

NON-FLYING JOBS

Most air force jobs are on the ground. There are hundreds of non-flying jobs that keep each pilot and aircraft in the air. These jobs include air traffic controllers, mechanics, cooks, medics and drivers.

A pilot trains on a flight simulator.

A "yellow shirt" aircraft director signals a pilot on an aircraft carrier.

GLOSSARY

accelerate – to increase in speed.

airspace – the air (sky) above a country in which aircraft can fly. Each country controls its airspace and says which aircraft can fly there.

altitude – the height of an aircraft above the ground.

briefing – a meeting to give accurate information to someone about a situation.

cargo – the goods or items carried on an aeroplane, ship or motor vehicle.

coordination – being able to make your body and senses work well together. For example, when a pilot's eyes see danger, the pilot's hands must react fast on the aircraft's controls.

cyclone – a violent storm that rotates quickly and has very strong winds.

detect – to discover or notice something.

evade – to try to escape or avoid someone or something.

first responder – a person (such as a police officer or firefighter) who is trained to arrive first in an emergency and provide help.

ground crews – the non-flying members of an air force. They take care of the aircraft.

infrared cameras – cameras that "see" the heat of objects and translate it into a photograph.

intelligence – information about the enemy or enemy activities. It is usually secret.

magnitude – the strength of an earthquake represented by a number based on the earthquake's waves.

NATO – the North Atlantic Treaty Organisation, a group of countries that have agreed to provide protection and security to one another.

oxygen – an invisible gas in the air that people need to breathe to stay alive.

parachute – a large piece of thin cloth used to make a person or object fall more slowly; to jump using a parachute.

personnel – the people who work for an organisation.

radar – a way to detect (see left) distant objects. Radar can work out an object's position and speed by sending radio waves that reflect off the object's surfaces.

stealth technology – technology that makes an aircraft almost invisible to radar (see above). A stealth plane has special panels that absorb radar waves instead of reflecting them.

INDEX

A
air-to-air missiles 20
air forces 4-5
aircraft 20-21, 22-23, 24-25, 28-29
Airspace Control Alert (ACA) 7, 14

B
B-21 Raider 24-25

C
C-17 transport plane 12-13
C-5M Super Galaxy 29
CH-47 Chinook 28-29
Chetak helicopters 11
Combat Air Patrol (CAP) 26
cyclone (Chennai, India) 10-11, 31

E
earthquake (southern Turkey) 12-13
emergency help 10-11, 12-13

F
F-35 fighter jet 20-21
fighter planes 7, 20-21, 22-23, 24-25, 26-27
flying gear 15
fuel 21, 26-27

G
g-force 18-19
g-pants 15, 18
Gripen fighter jet 22-23
ground crews 6-7, 9, 30-31

H
helmet 15, 21

L
low-level flying 16

N
natural disasters 5, 10-11, 12-13

P
parachute 5, 29, 31
pilots 4-5, 7, 8-9, 14-15, 16-17, 18-19, 21, 25, 30

Q
Quick Reaction Alert (QRA) 7, 14

R
radar 16, 24, 31
RAF Airbus A400M Atlas 5

S
scramble 7, 8
sortie 14
speed (of planes) 8-9, 16, 22
stealth technology 24, 31

T
tanker plane 26
training 14, 16-17, 30

U
United States Air Force (USAF) 12, 29

Picture credits:
(t=top; b=bottom; m=middle; l=left; r=right):
Shutterstock: Zieusin 1bg; Mike Mareen 4bg; Martin Hibberd 5bg; PeopleImages.com – Yuri A 6b; Michael Derrer Fuchs 7t; Apiguide 7b; Soos Jozsef 8m; Ryan Fletcher 9bg; Lakeview Images 11tr; VanderWolf Images 13tr, 21br; ANURAKE SINGTO-ON 14m; PW.Stocker 15bg; Bekirevren 17bg; Noraismail 19bg; Jgorzynik 20b; Anette Holmberg 22-23bg; Sergii Figurnyi 24br; Alaskagirl8821 22bl; Mike Mareen 24t; Thomas D Dittmer 25bg; ChameleonsEye 26m; Peter R Foster IDMA 27bg; Isak Wold 29b; George Xu 29tl; Kojihirano 28b; Derek Gordon 30br; Lerner Vadim 30bl; Sam-whitfield1 16m; Aappp 2-3bg; Plsantanu 10-11bg; Rebius 12-13.

Every effort has been made to trace the copyright holders, and we apologise in advance for any unintentional omissions. We would be pleased to insert the appropriate acknowledgements in any subsequent edition of this publication.